Protecting Preloved B

BOOK of FL

PPBC educate owners to the risks associated with offering their Border Collies *Free to a Good Home*, and about the dangers of these dogs being used as bait within the dog fighting community. We organise support for owners and suggest additional options such as the use of our fostering / adoption programme.

Protecting Preloved Border Collies
Charity Number 1166458

All About PPBC ...

Protecting Preloved Border Collies (PPBC) is established in England and Wales and recognised by HM Revenue and Customs as a registered Charity (Number 1166458). We work tirelessly for the welfare of Border Collies. We have a strict policy of never putting a physically or mentally healthy dog to sleep, thereby ensuring that, if an owner requires our assistance, we will safeguard their dog's welfare right from the onset.

Members of the public often believe that, by offering their collie for free, they are giving their dog a better chance of finding a loving, forever home. Unfortunately, the opposite is actually true. By educating the public through warning messages and offers of support, we are often able to minimise the trauma of 'the unknown' whilst empowering the owners to make suitable choices for their loved pet.

Protecting Preloved Border Collies arranges and coordinates the transportation of border collies, oversees home-checks and has a database of fosterers and adopters. We are steadily building a network of key contacts and organisations and our membership is growing daily.

We are horrified at what's happening out there but we can make a difference!

If you want to help then please let Protecting Preloved Border Collies know ... we need enough people to care to be able to reach those *free to good home* border collies that are totally dependent on us to step in and protect them.

Website: www.protectingprelovedbordercollies.co.uk
Email: protectingprelovedbordercollies@yahoo.com
Facebook: www.facebook.com/protectingprelovedbordercollies

How it began ...

PPBC was initially set up early in 2012 to message *free to good home* ads regarding the danger of free collies being used as bait by the dog fighting community. We would send out standard messages warning owners of the dangers. If those placing adverts approached us for help we would endeavour to find a placement in a Border Collie rescue for their dog.

Originally it was thought that the sole problem for the Border Collies in this situation was the dog fighting community but as we became more involved in the *free to good home* advert situation a bigger picture started to emerge.   After setting-up the Protecting Preloved Border Collies facebook page we found an ever-increasing number of owners desperate for help.

The group is run by collie lovers and we all knew that if a collie is placed in a home that isn't suited to him/her, with owners that don't understand the needs of a Border Collie things do go wrong.   Behavioural problems emerge in the collie and things spiral downwards.

In desperation, the owner can't cope and decides to re-home by advertising it as *free.* Then someone sees the advert and thinks they would quite like a collie and as it's free they'll get it.   But in a new environment the dog is confused/scared/stressed and the behavioural problems escalate because the new owner doesn't know what to do. This can lead to a collie being kept in a way that is totally unsuitable or the collie is re-advertised again for free ... and so it goes on in a never-ending cycle of misery/fear and stress for a dog that is highly intelligent.

There are also many owners that love their collie but life happens, relationship breakdown, illness, relocation, working hours change etc., which may make it impossible for them to keep their collie. These owners are heartbroken at having to re-home their beloved pet and often rescues are too full to help so what else can they do but try to find them a new home.

These owners truly believe that their dog has a better chance of finding a loving home by offering them *free* because more people would be willing to take it. They are shocked when they realize the dangers.

Many remove their advert or ask for a payment.

Some ask for more help.

Initially we were facilitators in finding rescue placements for these collies but as we grew we began developing a network of fosterers and adopters right across the UK. Each fosterer or adopter is fully processed and home-checked plus we match the collie to the home ensuring as much as possible that the needs of both the collie and the fosterer/adopter are met. We also run a closed group on Facebook for all fosterers and adopters to enable them to get support when needed.

Each and every Collie that comes into Protecting Preloved Border Collies has lifetime back up from the Charity. Health care in the form of neutering, micro chipping, vaccinating, worming and defleaing ... plus any other health issue which needs investigation is covered when they enter our system. We do not use a kennelling system and each collie is assessed by collie savvy fosters in their own homes prior to being available for adoption.

Protecting Preloved Border Collies endeavours to save as many collies as they possibly can.

As we grew we were also asked to take Collies from pounds that are under a seven-day put to sleep order if a rescue does not take them, or they are reclaimed by their original owners. It is also not unknown for Vet's to contact us directly if they consider a physically and mentally healthy collie brought in to be put-to-sleep is just in the wrong environment.

In late August 2012, we started the process to become a recognized charity and registered status was approved.

Protecting Preloved Border Collies
Charity Number 1166458

PPBC FURRY FAILS ... Club Members

GUNNAR

My furry boy's story (Wendy Perry)

It was May 2013 when we lost our girl, Cerys to bladder cancer. My daughter and I were adamant that we wouldn't have another dog and put ourselves through that pain again.

But the house was so quiet, no waggy tail for us when we got home from work and we missed the walks so much, and the face washes we'd had from Cerys.

So, we applied to PPBC to foster. The two we felt that would be ideal were Toby and Lola but as happens sometimes in rescue the foster dogs needed to be swapped around so we were asked if we would take Gunnar instead.

He came to us all the way from Scotland and what a sorry sight he was.

He had his mat which unfortunately was more holes than mat, a postman Pat toy, two tug-toys and his Manchester United lead, which to this day he still has because although he doesn't like it on he does like to carry it.

From that very first day I lost my seat and was relegated to sit on the other chair. We spent hours talking to each other, he was so funny. He could imitate my mouth and he made such funny noises when he was talking. It was for all-the-world as if we were having a confab.

We'd been fostering him for a couple of months and I had a message from a lady who was interested in adopting him. I went into a panic.

I contacted PPBC admin to let them know someone was interested in him. I didn't want to let this lad with the bouncy run that looks like a baby deer with straight legs go.

I was in such a state and crying he had crept into our hearts.

Admin rang me and asked if we wanted to let him go. Definitely not, I told them WE needed that funny little boy in OUR lives.

Strangely enough he must have known because although he's a right Mummies boy now he can twist us all around his paws.

He'd like to be with us 24/7 (but we have to sleep sometimes, even if he's on the bed).

My sister thinks he's the cutest black and white collie ever and as she leaves our house and we're saying 'bye-bye' he is running to the door and then back to us, barking and waiting for kisses.

I've never known such a good boy.

Bryn's story (Karen Janes)

My name is Bryn. It used to be Ben but mum and dad wanted me to have a special name when they decided I could come and live with them forever. Bryn is the Welsh version of Ben. It means hill and we live on one so it was the perfect new name for me for my new home!

This is my story.

I was born on a farm in Wales but I don't really remember that. I am a Border Collie with a little bit of English Springer Spaniel (I think that just means my ears are a bit confused and possibly my brain too!).

When I left the farm I went to live with a family who had some small people. They lived in a flat in a town and didn't have a garden but they used to take me for walks to the park and they tried their best for me. As I got a bit older, going to the park wasn't really enough exercise for me and I started to feel a bit cooped up at home. Some building work started and it got noisy, which I didn't like, so I barked and jumped around a lot. My family decided that they couldn't really give me what I needed so they asked the kind people at PPBC to find someone else to look after me.

Mum and Dad came to collect me in the summer time when I was 18 months old. They seemed like nice people so I was happy to go with them. I dragged them all the way to their car where I met Juno for the first time. She was sitting in the boot and looked a bit scared. Mum and Dad asked me to get in the crate next to Juno. I couldn't quite stand up properly, and I like to stand up and look where we're going; I think I was a bit bigger than what they were expecting! I don't have to travel in the crate anymore as I am so good in the car; I get to look out the window all the time.

I wasn't sure if Juno was pleased to see me or not but I soon understood that she gets scared about lots of things, especially when they're new. Mum and Dad were fostering me because they wanted to find another dog who could help Juno feel more relaxed and confident, especially when they needed to go out. She really does worry A LOT so they wanted to make sure they found the right one. At last I had found my opportunity: I could be 'Super Bryn to the rescue'. I always knew I was destined to be a superhero! Secretly Mum and Dad said that they decided I could stay forever after less than a week but they wanted to be sure because Juno had turned out to have lots more problems than they thought. They were also worried they couldn't help two dogs at once. What they didn't understand, until later, was that I had come to help them!

I started to really like my new home. I liked having Juno to play with and we live in the country so there are lots of fields to run around in. I missed my small people a bit but there are some hooman pups who live in our street, and even the one who is scared of dogs has started to love me, especially now I practice being calm when we meet people outside. Mum and Dad took us for long walks and then started taking me to Juno's puppy school too. It took me a while to get used to being with lots of other dogs but I got the hang of it. As I was settling, I started to worry that I might have to move again. I thought I should make sure I worked my magic on Mum and Dad so that they would discover that I am a superhero in disguise.

One day Juno got something called a season. Mum and Dad thought that they should leave us separately when they went out, so they shut me behind something called a baby gate – how rude!! Juno got really worried and started chewing on the door frame. Well, there was only one thing for a superhero to do: I broke through the baby gate (which is the only time I have ever did that, until I learnt to jump over it that is - but that is a whole other story!). I rushed to tell Juno that it was ok and that Mum and Dad would be home soon. I think that might be what clinched it for me. Mum and Dad said that although Juno had chewed some more of the door frame she was much less upset than last time, because I was with her. They were so impressed that I had rescued her that they signed some forms and they stopped being foster mum and dad and became just mum and dad.

Although mum and dad now know that I am Super-Bryn the good thing about them is that they noticed that although I'm brave I also get a bit worried sometimes too. They make sure I get lots of fuss and special time with them. They love me for helping Juno who had lots of horrible things happen to her, but they also love me because I'm so amazing and funny and affectionate and have lots of different expressions; well, who wouldn't love me?

Mum says I am an extrovert and I love meeting people and getting cuddles and having my chin stroked. I LOVE treats and I have lots of other doggy friends who come walking with us, and sometimes come to stay. Now I'm learning to do agility and I've learnt how to relax properly so I hardly bark at all, except at the postman but I think that's a good job to do. I still get a bit distracted sometimes and worried when other dogs come near me on the lead but I'm practising lots not to be. I get to go to the pub where they give us chews and I visit all the people in our village who are in my fan club, you can join if you like?

We sometimes stop at the café and meet lots of people and I like to go swimming in the river, especially when Mum and Dad throw treats in. We sometimes go to stay at granny's and I love running around her garden and on the beach.

We've just started going on holiday in our new campervan. I hadn't seen one of those before but I love it because we travel around and stay in fields and mum and dad are with us all the time. I'm very good and like to sleep in the space under the bed, but in the morning I always get up and climb onto mum and dad because I know they appreciate an early morning wakeup call on holiday!

I've lived with mum and dad and Juno for a year and half now so I just turned three and I think that means I'm a big boy. Most of all I love being with mum and dad because their hands are gentle. Some of the hoomans I've met didn't have gentle hands and that makes me worry sometimes so I think I'll stay here forever. I'm glad PPBC helped mum and dad to find me, they're very lucky.

Glen – The Next Chapter

Well you've probably read all about my arrival.

You haven't?
Then you really need
to get the first book.
Protecting Preloved
Border Collies
Fury Tails

Well anyway, after couple of weeks arriving on English soil I had to move into another foster home. Unsure of where I was going after being picked up and taken on yet another journey it was all getting a bit confusing. But in this home, I was getting unusual attention.

This woman had a brush thing.

I did look rather large, so much so they had a fund-raising completion on how much I weighed, which raised a few quid. Well whoever said I was 35kg was wrong. I wasn't a wannabe Malamute at all Auntie Von. It was ALL fur. 25kg slim Jim.

Just so you know, I don't like having baths, I hate them. It takes two folks to get me in.

On walks I saw lots of cars, trucks and, favorite of all trailers. Boy, did I want to chase them. I've never seen so many moving things before.

CHASE, Chase, chase … my foster mum said, 'NO' but I had to be kept on the lead all the time because I couldn't help myself. Where I used to be was very quiet. This was a whole new world.

We went on walks to the park, and the beach and I love to play with a ball. I love all toys. It's very rare you'll see me without anything in my mouth.

I Have other dogs to play with and they are all nice. Hector can be a bit bossy and watches me a lot. I think it's a man crush. Silly dog, but with me it goes straight over the ears.

So, this is me in my foster home. Brushed. Nice (!) bathed … Yuk! Sleeping arrangements. Anywhere I park myself, like the end of bed.

I think I'm not for moving again, so I need to put on my charm.

Note from mum. (Linda Tipping - Failed fosterer)

Glen moved in. Took over my bed, sofa, and my heart after one week. He's cuddly, affectionate and a charmer. He certainly knew how to play his cards.

He's still on a long line two years on as he still has a fetish for trailers, but is no longer interested in cars, buses, or trucks. His main problem is he's nosey and very easily distracted, but this is just him. Full of life and excited about the slightest thing, except raw carrot, he's a posh dog and needs his home cooking!

Now age 9. Here's to, hopefully another ten years with my overgrown puppy. I LOVE HIM TO THE MOON AND BACK!!

Fly & Amiera (Robbie Beechey)

As we get older and look at our canine family, we increasingly began to think about what might happen if they were to outlive us.

For most of us the thought that they might end up in rescue kennels, or even have to be put down is horrific, and so we try to ensure that our dogs are not so young that this is likely to happen.

By doing this though we create another situation that we don't like. We ourselves are faced with the prospect of having no canine companions just at the time of our lives when we have the time and energy to enjoy them and possibly have a real need for the love and company they give, yet we know that we probably won't be able to be there for them in another 10 - 15 years, so can't take on another young dog.

Unfortunately, old dogs are not easy to rehome, they can have expensive medical needs, they can't always keep up with the long walks prospective owners envisage. They will only have a short lifespan, so many rescues just do not take them in as they are likely to be stuck with them and then unable to help more dogs.

When we lost our last collie in 2015, we looked at our remaining two old boys and decided we would try to foster, or adopt elderly collies who, as they approached old age had lost their home - maybe because their owner had died or they'd had to move to sheltered accommodation.

Amiera and Fly found themselves in exactly that situation, their owner died very suddenly, leaving them, together with a much younger dog all alone. Amiera was 10 - exactly the right age range for us, so we applied to foster her with a view to adopt.

We fell in love with her at first sight - who wouldn't?

A beautiful, well behaved girl who only wanted to give and receive affection. She settled with our 2 boys straight away and proved an absolute delight from the start.

We soon realised though that part of the constant need for reassurance and affection was in fact her way of dealing with stress.

In the space of two weeks she'd lost her lifelong home, her owner, the two dogs she was living with ... and was now having to adjust to being in a new home, with 2 new dogs and people she didn't know and in completely different surroundings. She did her best, but she was naturally a confused dog.

Fly meanwhile had been described as around 6 years of age although those who saw her thought she looked much older - too young for us to adopt in all fairness to her, so she went off to a different foster home in Taunton. When she went for her first vet visit however it was confirmed that she was in fact an old dog, older than Amiera.

Discussing their progress with her foster mum I did say if only we'd known she was an oldie as well I would have happily taken them together.

Although she had fallen in love with Fly in the same way that we had with Amiera, Tina was finding that Fly too was very sad and confused, and very bravely made the decision that it would be better for both girls if they were reunited as soon as possible.

So, one week after they had been separated, Steve made the long trip from Lincolnshire down to Somerset to pick her up and bring her to us here in Yorkshire.

Poor Fly had no idea where she was and wouldn't move from her spot in the car, so Steve lifted Amiera in. It took a second or two for them to realise what was happening but the moment it dawned on them that they were together again was one of the most moving things I have ever seen.

They licked each other's faces, pressed their bodies together and both then refused to move out of the car. When Steve lifted Amiera out Fly came to be lifted down too.

They have stuck together like Siamese twins ever since and are settling very well into their new life with us. It was so easy to fall for Fly's charms, this brave old girl clearly had some physical discomfort but her tail never stops wagging. For us too it seemed that she was destined to be very special to us.

We lost a short haired collie at the age of 10 in 2007, so missed out on her old age. Fly is so like her in appearance and in character that it almost feels as though Tag has been returned to us and we can now enjoy the years that we missed. Fortunately, like Tag, Fly is a strong character who retains her individuality – like Tag, yes – but carbon copy, definitely not.

When Amiera came she had a limp and was found to have an arthritic wrist. However, after treatment the limp disappeared and hasn't returned. Fly though is very arthritic. Medication is helping and she's walking better but as is always the case with arthritis some days are better than others. She's in the right place for her walks though, very flat landscape, elderly dogs to walk with and we've lots of time to do it at her pace as we too are elderly.

Fly is becoming much more confident now, happy to do her own thing and coping well with new experiences, though she will still make sure she's close to Amiera if anything worries her.

Amiera on the other hand is still very insecure and reverts to extreme puppy behaviour if she's worried, licking Fly's mouth much to Fly's disgust, but it is very early days yet and, unsurprisingly separation anxiety still affects them both.

Only time and consistency will resolve that for them – imagine if children, or adults for that matter had gone through the same experiences. At the very least they'd have had counselling and possibly much more.

Usually animals are expected to get on with it as best they can.

That apart, they are take anywhere dogs, as we can be quite confident that they will behave perfectly. They love going out, meeting people and other dogs and will happily lie quietly while we gossip or stop for coffee.

We adopted the pair of them as soon as we possibly could and are now enjoying watching them come to terms with their new life in their new family.

We are so lucky that these two lovely dogs have come to live with us, and though it means that there might not be any more foster dogs (we hope that the 4 living here now are going to be around for a while), we couldn't be happier that we've failed as foster parents.

And then we were 5 ...

Sophie

She's such a sweet little dog.

She came to us aged 13, a couple of months after Fly and Amiera because her previous fosterer was hospitalised.

When she arrived, she was poorly and obviously traumatised by the sudden upset to her life.

It took her a while to settle but now she is just one of the family.

She enjoys pottering about, hydro sessions, walks and just being with canine and human company all the time.

Work, Rest & Play

A fortune can be spent on toys ...
(but that's often just not what they really want to play with)

Wisp ... Please don't throw it through my window!
(Lynn Gaspar)

My Friend WISP

 Let me introduce myself, my name is Jessica Parker Brown, Jessie for short and I am a blue merle. I am going to tell you a story about a lad I was privileged to know and love called Wisp.

Affectionately known as Wispy Woo.

At the end of 2012 Protecting Preloved Border Collies were asked to help the most handsome tri colour Collie called Wisp. He was a fully trained working sheepdog who took his commands in Welsh. I watched my mum drawl over him….and if I'm honest I did too, but heard her say 'with everything going on he can't come here, the times not right'.

Christmas passed and early in the new year a car arrived in the yard. Wisp's fosterers had driven him down to West Sussex to meet a potential adopter but he didn't want to take commands from them, so it wasn't going to work and he accompanied them on a pre-arranged visit to head office. Wow!!!! Was he good looking!!!! When he got out of the car and met Mum he did everything she asked so even though the time still wasn't right he stayed on the farm with us.

Fate had taken a hand.

Wisp loved buckets, his football, sheep and ME (he did love our mum too).

He would put his head in a bucket and toss it up into the air, it really made a racket and I wasn't too sure about that.

I adored him and if he was lying in the yard and Mum didn't let me out, I would just go through the cat flap to find him.

He played chase with me and let me get away with blue murder even letting me steal his bones and toys.

Fate again took a twist and Wisp was destined to be heading back to his homeland with Mum and the rest of us.

On the day we left for the new farm in Wales, Wisp and I travelled in the truck with Mum, the other dogs went in cars with friends and relatives. It was a long journey for me, I'd never travelled that far but Wisp was a seasoned traveller and with him beside me I was reassured. Nothing ever phased Wisp, he was such a brave boy.

When we reached Wales, Mum was able to help a lot more PPBC dogs and Wisp was very good at teaching those that weren't very confident how to be so, dogs like Bob and Skye G benefitted from his behaviour.

In November 2015 Wisp became ill and visited the vet who like Mum didn't know what was wrong with him so blood tests were taken. One minute he would be lethargic and the next almost back to normal. He was a dog that loved life and Mum to the full and was never a dog to give in. He fought the illness to the end but the tumour on his liver had ruptured and Wisp passed over Rainbow bridge. Mum cried lots and we all missed him and still do. Mum says that one day we will meet him again. I really hope so, he was my best friend.

Dillon (Stephanie Young)

Dillon came into the rescue from a pound on 3rd October 2014 as he was due to be PTS that day. There was no history known about him but we soon found out he was not used to living indoors as he feared the TV, vacuum cleaner etc., in fact he was scared of most things. We coaxed him indoors but he spent many night sleeping by the front door. He didn't interact much. He was a bag of bones, weighing in at only 10kg, matted and covered in oil.

He followed me everywhere, watching me constantly but showed us that he could get on with our other Border collies and our Jack Russel Terrier. We decided he must stay and adopted him within weeks of him coming here as we felt that Dillon had already been through enough.

These days he is a healthy weight and although he still has fear-related issues with strange dogs he is perfectly settled at home in his own pack. He is my constant shadow and never leaves my side. He has learnt sit, wait, paw plus many more commands and sleeps next to our bed, no longer needing to be constantly by the front door. We couldn't want for a better dog, he never puts a foot wrong. He is a happy confident lad these days, is passionate with his cuddles and loves his comforts. He is now where he belongs and has been the inspiration to many of my poems.

Never give up on me

Stephanie Young

Bad memories spook me from time to time,
I may not share them but that's no crime,
They creep up on me when I least expect,
They are scary and have a bad effect,
I see your face and see your hand,
I hear your soft words and I understand,
But that man beside you reminds me of the past,
Let me get over this moment ... it won't last.
A day or two and I will be back to trusting,
I just need to take some time, I need to do some adjusting,
It was just a shaky moment I had when I saw him,
I just had a flashback, a shaking limb.
I know I can trust you but so I really dare,
I know you care, but I hate how people glare.
I know you will protect me forever and a day,
But some days are black and others are grey.
I stand beside you or behind you when I'm scared,
But trust is 98% ... not whole as I'm always prepared.

But please never give up on me,
Because I want to forget ... I want to be free.

Bad memories creep up when I least expect,
They fill me with terror they have an effect.
It may seem like I don't trust you and never could,
But I will ... one day ... I know I should.
But for now, allow me my time,

It's not a lot to ask ... it's not a crime,
I just need to watch, listen, and hear,
One day I will be free and everything will be clear.

But Please Never give up on me,
Because I want to forget ... I want to be free.

So, if I run off and stare at you,
It's not because I am stubborn or I don't have a clue,
I maybe having a flash-back of things that happened before,
I may be remembering ... that bang of the door.
I cannot tell you how I feel,
But the for me those shaky moments are real,
I try to forget and I'm getting slowly there,
You know I am as I sit next to you on the chair,
But learning to trust is the hardest things I do,
For Trust is something I never knew
Trust, Love, Caring, Sharing, Tenderness, I have never felt,
My life ... before ... was just a leather belt.
So, I'm sorry if I have wobbly days,
When I run, cower, or stand in a gaze
It is not you, it's a memory I cannot share,
It's a dark memory ... yes, I know you care.

But Please NEVER give up on me.
Because I want to forget ... I WANT to be FREE.

Balian's Story (Caroline O'Hare)

Hello, I am Balian, a 6-year-old Collie x German Shepherd.

I was born in a farm and went to live with my family when I was a puppy. My family loved me lots, in fact I was a bit spoilt too. I loved playing with my Kong, watching TV from my crate, learning lots of tricks and going for walks with mum. Life was good. Then, when I was almost four years old everything changed. Mum was no longer with me all the time, I was being left on my own a lot and was getting distressed.

PPBC stepped in and said they would find me a new home. A few weeks later I went on a very long car journey with all my things, two huge bags full of toys and treats, plus my crate and a long, handwritten letter from mum.

Several hours later we arrived at a new place with lots of countryside smells. My new Foster Mum greeted me so warmly that I put my ears back, wiggled my back side and jumped up to say my first hello. There was a very strange, thin, gentle long legged girl dog that lived there, Sylvie the greyhound. Later foster dad arrived and he was okay too.

This was all so strange, new and scary and I couldn't really understand what was happening. I couldn't stop drinking water, panting, and having wees (in the garden of course) and I wouldn't settle, worried they may leave me on my own again.

I tried to be on my best behaviour and as the days went by I relaxed a bit. I learned the rules and tried very hard to be good, but whenever I got anxious I would switch off and start air snapping, barking and chasing my tail. "He is a handful, he's hyper, barks a lot, has separation anxiety and other issues typical of working collies" I heard Foster Mum say, "but nothing we can't deal with, he really wants to please and I think he'll enjoy doing Working Trials".

Just three weeks after I arrived, I was adopted. Mum had said she wanted a challenge and I made sure she got one!

However, I started to become increasingly reactive to other dogs. Although I am fine on lead, walking side by side with other dogs, I find it very difficult to cope if other dogs are running around. I just don't know how to relate to them and even lunge and bark at some, bullying any that are a bit afraid of me. I do love greyhounds and lurchers though, as they run fast and I like chasing them.

We started training shortly after I arrived and I loved it. I am very focused on mum when we're training, and when I see her get the tracking harness out or the dumbbell I get so excited. I am never happier than when I have a job to do and if getting things right it means treats or a play with my tug! Unfortunately, I now have an injury in one of my front legs (due to jumping and twisting to catch a ball), so I won't be able to do Working Trials after all, as I can't do the jumps.

Sylvie went to the Bridge earlier this year and I miss her lots. I never appreciated how much I relied on her when facing scary things, such as traffic. So, now I am getting used to being an only dog. Mum and Dad say I will have a new play-mate at some point, but we need to make sure I've calmed down a bit more first.

Mum says it's been a long journey and I'm still Work in Progress, but also that I'm the most rewarding dog she's ever had and that she's learned more about dog behaviour and training than she had in over 30 years of previously owning dogs ... plus she loves me to bits!

Nellie and Frost (Fiona Alto)

We joined the foster group of PPBC to adopt a specific dog as company for our 2yr old farm bred Border collie, Scoutie. Unfortunately, the dog we wanted wasn't available so we sat back and waited, we didn't have to wait long as when a collie x spaniel popped up needing a foster placement we offered her a place.

Nellie bounced into our lives on the 22/08/13. She made herself right at home and Scoutie was happy with her being there. She was supposed to be 4yr old but was probably more like 9+. However, she wasn't what we were specifically looking for, that sounds awful but I was wanted your stereotypical black and white long coated border collie bitch and she was the complete opposite a mid-coated merle X breed but in hindsight, it only took a couple of days to decide we were keeping her. Sometimes you have to admit defeat and go with what's best for the resident dogs, the dog you have in foster care and your heart. She is a beautiful girl and we simply fell in love with her.

One evening I was sat doing not much and two 14-week-old puppies popped up on the PPBC group page needing foster places. One was traditional black and white, named Ollie and a white boy with black spots and face mask called Gwyn. I pounced, I actually wanted Ollie however, it was thought he had a high prey drive so as we have cats we got Gwyn.

When we collected him from transport run he'd had a terrible journey. He'd been travel sick and had the runs, so was caked in faeces and urine. He stank!

We took him home let him settle in and fed him and let him sleep, but early the next morning when I got up I had never seen such a mess, never had I had a dog or puppy even soil their own bed but

he had gone for extreme total carnage. It was at that point it was decided that I would sleep downstairs with him, which I did for three months.

It became evident in the first week Frost, as we had re-named him wasn't going anywhere. It was a love story ... he needed me and I needed him, we were inseparable and he was my life. Everything else fell by the wayside. He was not quite right, not the full shilling as my mum would say. There was something missing. We had so many tests done as his behaviour escalated and spiralled out of control but nothing really ever showed up. He had allergies, partial fits and his eyes never focused correctly, however we loved him.

Life was put on hold. We walked alone at the crack of dawn to keep him safe but as his behaviour escalated and his allergies got worse to the point where he lived on steroids and medication. He was ferocious with kids, disliked most people even those he saw regularly, and would let people into the house but woe betide them if they wanted to move. But with us he was the perfect little boy, loveable, kind, funny and an absolute angel. He just couldn't cope in the real world. It was all too much for him to deal with ... but we still loved him. It's hard looking back on it all.

One fateful day we went to sort the caravan out at the coast. I wish we had never gone, I really do. We went early to avoid traffic and left the dogs at home. When we got back we put the dogs in the car and set off out as it was a glorious day. We thought we'd take them for a paddle but didn't really think it through. It was quite where we'd gone, but then a mother turned up with her son and their dog. Frost went ballistic, we left the pond but they followed. Frost was going mental, we diverted off again they followed we turned round, we looked back they'd turned around. It was as if they were trying to send Frost over the edge of reason, eventually we lost them but by doing that we were in a busier part of the park, that just sent Frost spiralling out of control and then he flipped and hit the floor. We got him home and he slept, we took him to the vets and he continued to sleep. He didn't wake up.

I will cry forever about Frost and that fateful day. I'd have done anything to alter the course of that day. I'd have done anything to follow him over the rainbow bridge. We love you Frost, you were and always will be the love of my life!

Still here ...

Lee Montgomery-Hughes

You caught me out today
You showed that you're still here
I wasn't quite expecting you to stay so very near

You're greeted by the others, though all I see is space
They know more than I, that you never left this place
You make your lead now tumble, untouched down to the floor
As we're getting ready for the walks you all adore
You'll leave some extra footprints when the weather is so wet
I still put out your food bowl, I just seem to forget

But you caught me out today
By proving you're still here
You never really left me ... I now see that crystal clear

Sheba and Jazz (Geoff Rone)

Jazz's Tail

It was just before Christmas when Dad sat down on the sofa next to me and Mum sat on her chair. I can still remember how it went.

Dad said, "Listen, in a couple of days a new little dog called Sheba is coming to stay, probably for a few weeks".

Mum butted in, "Don't worry, if you don't like her she won't stay even that long".

This was a relief; I could cope for a few hours like when Noodle comes to visit.

Anyway, it was Christmas so I forgot all about the whole thing – I got a new rope knotty thing and an antler chew that was rubbish and some other stuff that I ate.

On Monday 28th December – I'll never forget that date; Dad put *The Crate* up under the kitchen work top, "Hello" I thought, "somethings going on, I sleep over there by the radiator". I forgot about it and had my morning nap till the phone rang and Dad said it was 'The Transporter' and she'll be here in half an hour.

One of my Super Powers is recognising when the grown-ups are a bit excited and I spotted it then. I spotted it even more when Dad put my lead on and we went out THROUGH THE FRONT DOOR! I only go out through the FRONT DOOR when Mike takes me on my holidays but Mike wasn't there, instead a lady was there with a smelly little dog. Well, naturally I barked at her like you do and I carried on barking when Mum took hold of this smelly dog's lead and WENT OFF WITH HER!

I wasn't having any of that so Dad and me followed them and walked along a bit then walked on opposite sides of the road and round the block and I was dead interested and barked some more then we headed home AND MUM BROUGHT THE SMELLY DOG TOO!

Well, Mum went through the side gate with Smelly Dog and Dad took me into the kitchen through the front door (still no sign of Mike) but Mum and smelly dog were the other side of the French doors in The Garden.

Now, I'm not precious about The Garden at all, it's a great place to trash stuff and skid about in the mud and I've had other friends to stay and play so I didn't mind seeing Smelly Dog there but Mum had her on a lead so Dad kept me on mine, then Mum moved up to the chair thing on the first terrace and sat on it with smelly dog and Dad took me out into the garden.

Well I don't mind telling you, it was a bit like walking on egg shells – broken egg shells that I'd broken, a delicate little sniff and a play with the ball then another sniff then we went inside and I was a bit rough and barky.

Dad said, "I'd better phone Rose and let her know she's OK".

Now I don't know who this Rose is but whatever she said must have been magic because Dad said that she said, "Just let them get on with it!"

Sheba's Tail

I'm quite good at looking small and delicate and do a really good "pathetic" if you know what I mean, so it came as a bit of a surprise to be put in a van and driven thousands of miles to a new country and everything.

I was actually quite innocent and hadn't done very much apart from have a litter of pups.

Anyway, one day in the winter this lady drove me for ages, she made me sit separate from her dogs because SHE said I was smelly and scratched a lot! The cheek!

Anyway, after ages I got out of the van and met another lady and this man was in the front garden with a big, stupid looking, barky dog.

To be honest, I was a bit worried and probably neurotic – even neurotic-ker than usual because I was in a new place and it was all very strange – I didn't have my puppy or my mum so I pretended to be really subdued and well behaved – just in case.

Anyway, the new lady took me for a walk and the barky dog came too. This was all a bit interesting and I'm not really that "into" interesting – I prefer a quiet life except where cats and birds are concerned.

We walked for ages till I was walking quite close to Barky Dog then we went back to new lady's house and she took me into the garden.

It looked like a big playground with mud and stuff to jump on and off.

After a bit the lady let me off my lead and barky dog and me sniffed each other like you do, but he was a real pain in the bum and just wanted to be all bouncy and play so I joined in a bit but stayed near to the new lady.

Jazz's Tail

Oh wow, she smelled brilliant!

Just like one of Dad's socks wrapped in bacon! So, I followed her around and she head butted at me a bit but mostly she stayed close to Mum, so in the end I made sure I claimed the sofa – it's my day bed. She had her tea in the crate and I had mine in my usual place then we went into the lounge and she stayed with Mum on her lead and I sat on the sofa with Dad – it was really civilised, she came over and banged my nose with her nose a few times but she wasn't too bad and after a quick walk outside we went to bed – brilliant, she was locked in the crate and I slept next to her. She whinged a bit till I heard Mum come downstairs and go into the lounge then she only whimpered quietly......all night.

Sheba's Tail

Well, yes I was a bit pathetic that first night – actually probably for the first three weeks but I have "issues" with separation and I really need to know that I'm secure. Anyway, the next morning, the big man came into the kitchen and let me out of my bedroom – the dog who is called Jazz swapped a big plastic bone for a biscuit and I got one too! Then he opened the back door so I could go and have a wee and Jazz came out as well and I followed him up to green muddy bit called The Lawn and started to play a kind of hide and seek game with him. We did this for ages and it got a bit rough and tumble and suddenly I realised that this could be fun and things might work out. We played and played and we got wet and muddy but this seemed to be OK with everybody. I learned that Jazz was big and strong but I was much faster and more nimble and he liked to be chased. The man and the lady called us down and made a fuss of us and she dried me – I got a bit jealous of Jazz getting dried by the man but I soon learned that "we all love each other in this house".

And you know what? That last bit's true. Except for the cats!

The Man and The Lady's Tale

Our vet confirmed that she did have a minor skin problem when she arrived and this coupled with a serious lack of exercise had possibly caused her "bad smell". A few weeks of horrendous non-stop rain, running in the field and a change in diet seemed to solve that problem.

She went into season ten days after arriving so making any kind of accurate assessment was going to be difficult. PPBC Admin agreed that the Foster Period could be extended into the second month but in all honesty, it was too late by then. We'd been suckered in by this lightning fast little girl who gives the soppiest collie cuddles you can imagine and she wasn't going anywhere.

Sprocket (Julia Bertram)

Brrrring-brrring. Brrrring-brrring. "Hello?"

"Hi, this is Lynn from the PPBC, you've recently passed your home check with regards to fostering a border collie for us."

"Yes, that right.

"Well, we have been asked to take a young male, un-neutered and according to the Post Code given, he's about 10 miles from you. Are you able to help?"

"Of course, please send me the details."

It was getting dark on that Tuesday evening in November 2012 when I left a city centre property, handover papers signed and a fourteen-month-old border collie in tow. Or rather I was being towed. There were two reasons given for Sprocket's release into the care of the PPBC, his constant barking annoyed the neighbours and, they couldn't take him out as he pulled on the lead continually. As I walked to the car, I could vouch for the latter.

Hubby and son were thrilled that we had been accepted to foster and were waiting at home with our two other rescue collies (Not PPBC) for the new arrival. After introductions in the paddock that we rent from the local farmer, Heidi and Tyke accepted Sprocket as another displaced little dog, and our pack of three was formed.

"He's only here on a foster basis." I said. "So, don't get too attached."

His castration took place two days later, and the cone of shame made its appearance. Ten days later, the vet satisfied that everything was in order, Sprocket could be exercised.

Off to the paddock we went. It's about an acre and fully enclosed with good stock fencing. That boy ran and he ran and he ran. Would he come back when "Ball gone bed" was given as the command to stop? Oh no, he just kept running in big circles. Heidi and Tyke stood and watched. Much, much later, he had to stop, he was exhausted. The lead went on and we walked, to heel, the short distance to home.

This continued, twice a day for about two weeks until the penny dropped that he would get to go out and play again, when he was taken back to the house.

It didn't long for the vocals to start. Not Sprocket barking, there hadn't been so much as a muted woof from him. No, it was hubby and son.

"He can't go somewhere else now," they said. "He's settled here," they said.

I stood firm and said no, we're fostering. If we keep Sprocket, we won't be able to help the next wee soul that needs a safe place for a few weeks, but they were determined. "How can you let him go somewhere strange to him," they said. "He'll be confused all over again," they said.

Then came the email from Lynn asking for some up to date photographs of Sprocket as there was a potential adopter for him. Morphing into an Ostrich, I prevaricated. "Yes, I'll take some photos and send them to you. A few days later, another email. "Any photos?" Third email, "You do have the option to adopt him yourself."

Papers signed, fee paid.

"Phil, Bill? Ok, you win, Sprocket can stay."

To this day, hubby and son think that they wore me down … wrong, Sprocket stole my heart too.

Meet Megan (Sally Taphouse)

I fell in love with Megan the very first time I met her ... a very busy boisterous young lady at the time.

Megan was the first foster dog I had ever had. I saw her on the PPBC Facebook page and volunteered to take her, getting in just ahead of another volunteer.

I spoke to Lynn Gasper at length about her and we went through her owners' assessment. According to that, she was a perfect dog with no issues at all so I arranged to go and collect her from her home in Rochdale. It was a very long drive and the traffic was awful.

Her owners asked me in and introduced me to Megan, who was a very friendly dog that just wanted cuddles. They showed me all the tricks she could do, including emptying the washing machine and it was at that point that I realised that Megan was coming home with me to stay.

Her owner asked me if I was going to keep her but I just said maybe.

After a tearful goodbye and a long journey, we eventually arrived home. I introduced her to my 5 dogs, but unfortunately it was too late and dark to do long intro's, so they all just got thrown in at the deep end and although she didn't hit it off with all of them straight away, they all get on now.

She didn't sit or lay down for about 3 days, she was used to having a packet of Rich tea biscuits for treat so she was a bit hyper. She was also very overweight, had no manners around a ball or food, pulled like a train on the lead and stole anything, but she was a fast learner and driven, which was just what I wanted in a dog to be able to compete in Obedience and agility.

I signed her papers and paid my money within 4 weeks of her being here. That was two and a half years ago.

Today she is a very well-mannered highly motivated dog. She loves affection, her ball and her dinner. She has lost over 6kg and is super fit but still steals anything from the kitchen worktop if I happen to leave it in reach.

We haven't made it to any obedience competitions yet, but I'm sure she would do very well. She is a joy to have around and she has really found her forever home here.

Macey (Kerrylou Tempest)

Macey arrived as a foster dog and started to display those common signs of … 'Why am I not going home?' 'Why don't my family want me?' and 'What did I do wrong?'

She began to rebel, react, got short tempered, refused food and water, and became distant on walks. We even had an incident with another dog. Both were on leads when this dog came to say *hello*, one minute Macey is fine, the next she's is not. Heart-breaking is a huge understatement.

We've showered her with love, Ross took her on a treat spree to a pet store, we secured a field for her to hunt in, and started proper training. It's calmed her somewhat, but we're not out of the woods yet.

We decided to adopt her. She wasn't going to be able to cope with another move, but even if that wasn't an issue, she'd become my little wolfette companion, and I was not letting her go anywhere (good hot water bottles are hard to find - lol).

It's funny; after Lucky scattered over Rainbow Bridge we were adamant that a dog would never cross our threshold again, we had too much history with her, and I never thought I could love another dog even a fraction of how much I loved her. Then in comes Macey, with her silly fluffy tail, scatty barking, tongue baths, and a need to play tug at 3am every morning, and suddenly our hearts were stolen.

On the way to pick her up, I couldn't imagine life with Macey ... just 30 days later, and I couldn't imagine life without her. She really is my puppy love.

P.S.

I walked in on this scene earlier ... Lu is sat colouring, Macey is snuggled up next to her, and it just looked like the most natural thing ever.

Skye (Yvonne)

Nearing the end of March, on a sudden whim, Keith and I decided to dump ourselves onto Lynn Gaspar for a week. Upon arrival among the throng of hugs, licks, yelps and barks, there sat in the office a little shy, but loving bundle off Autumn coloured pom-pom fur that I'd never met one before.

A little Welsh Collie by the name of Skye and she was beautiful.

Throughout the week, I did my best to help out without getting in the way, but then there were times that I'd take myself through to the office and sit on the floor with Skye, both of us enjoying the moment.

I was leaning towards the thought that I'd never manage a dog full time again as my health is in limbo. I didn't think it fair to take on a dog, with my future unknown … but then isn't everybody's?!.

After a fun filled week, we returned to our dogless home, and world dominating cat. I would keep an eye on Skye's page and read whatever Lynn posted. Unbeknownst to me, Keith was doing the same.

On May the 4th, I casually mentioned Skye and showed Keith her latest picture. Keith remarked he had seen it, and he had been following her page … my eyebrows pricked up, this was unlike Keith to follow the wellbeing of a dog on social media. We had a chat about Skye, how she was, what she needed in a new home, how I'd manage to walk her if my hands were not great, what about work … what about, we tell Lynn we would like to consider Skye as our potential dog … I sent a message and Lynn duly got emotional.

Keith and I returned to Lynn's for a long weekend at the end of May and returned with our furry bundle. She has excelled herself in all areas. Initially she was scared of the car, traffic, loud noises that she couldn't see the source off, the cat, the postman, any dog that came near her, any stranger in the park. Within a week off becoming officially adopted at the end of June, she was let off leash for the first time. I had my heart in my mouth, this was a big step for her ... she loved it more than I did!

Many dog walkers have watched her grow in confidence at the park. She now actively seeks out people for attention, and approaches dogs with her pom-pom tail wagging. The postman loves her, Hermes delivery love her, the neighbours love her, Keith's camera club love her, our friends and family love her.

She has really come into her own. Now she will chase a ball ... OK, so she runs like Bambi on ice but it doesn't matter, she loves it and it makes me smile every time. She sits outside the kitchen waiting on me coming out, she follows me to the bin, she sneaks up onto the forbidden couch and Keith and I take turns in ensuring her belly is getting its daily quota of adequate rubbing. She gives paw with a swift and direct 33% angle shoot into the air ... almost like the Wehrmacht saluting the Fuehrer. She loves to paddle up to her belly, but hates a bath. She loves life and life is throwing all it can at her knowing she is soaking it up like a sponge.

Prior to this little girl making a home with us, I was not in a good place mentally, I'm still not, and will never be who I was. I used to avoid going out, outside was too peopley and dreaded plans of activity. Skye changed that, I now have no valid excuse for not going out and even when on my own, I have her by my side. The simple act of a lick up the side of my face is worth a thousand sayings of, " it will be OK".

Lynn reckons the reason she wasn't adopted was because she was waiting for me. I know that for whatever reason, she got under my heart and stayed there. Loved ones say, " oh, she's not like Tara ". Exactly, Tara was a one-off girl, as is this one. She lacks the stamina, the ball obsessive, the head strong manner, the determination of Tara. But she gives so much, and will give you her soul, which she has done to me and I promise to keep it safe. I do look at her and wonder who rescued who.

I'm not a believer of destiny or fate, but there is a reason she is mine and that reason is bigger than the both off us put together. I have lost so much in the last two years, more than most will ever truly know, but I've also gained so much back, and it's been because of Skye ... my Wee Welshy Wigglebum Skye.

FUNDRAISING ….

Amber's Walk

Amber came home from school one afternoon and said she would like to enter the "Tenner challenge " at school. She explained that she will be given £10 and she is to organise an event to raise money for a charity.

Amber chosen PPBC as her charity as that is where our dogs, Blue, Brogue, and Milo are from (all came as fosters, and all stayed).

She sat at the table all evening mind mapping different things she could do … these included cake sale, car wash, and lemonade stand, but she eventually decided she wanted to do a sponsored walk.

First, she approached the owner of the Parndon Mill hub of creativity to ask if she could use the hub as her start and finish point, as that would also offer car parking for anyone else that wanted to join her on the day.

This was all agreed and the date for the 5-mile walk was set for the 19th of March 2017.

Next, her mum set up a Facebook page and started advertising the walk. The support she received was amazing, with people wanting to sponsor her and join her on the walk. Amber got a message from co-op funeral care saying that they wanted to support her walk and offered to provide an ern, generator, tea and coffee, and bottled water for everyone taking part.

Amber received a letter from the House of Commons wishing her good luck with the sponsored walk inviting her on a tour round the Houses of Parliament.

This was amazing and saw a massive turning point where a little walk was now a big event. Amber was extremely excited about it.

The walk was a massive success with over 40 people and around 30 dogs turning up on the day to walk with amber. and her being able to raise over £2000.

Everyone involved in PPBC are <u>very</u> proud of her.

Volunteers are vital to all rescues.
Could You Help?

Everyone involved in this process are volunteers. The admin, organisers, and fundraisers give their time freely, the fosteres open their homes and their hearts to help the dogs and the transporters will often fund the run themselves.

If you would like to be involved please contact us via the website http://www.protectingprelovedbordercollies.org.uk

Also join us on FaceBook

Even if you are not in a position to be active within the rescue you can still help by simply *sharing* the posts about dogs that are looking for home.
www.facebook.com/protectingprelovedbordercollies

You can't teach an old dog new tricks

The saying might be a familiar one, but over time it has become more well-known for the idea of being so stuck in one way of doing something that it is not possible to adapt to anything else.

This, however is not always true …
Dogs of all ages can learn new things!

I'm an outdoor Collie
I'm used to my space,
I'm not used to people that get in my face.

I'm an outdoor Collie
I'm not used to noise
I don't like kids screaming or the sound of their toys

I'm an outdoor Collie
I have a Kennel and chain
I don't need a cute jacket, I quite like the rain

I'm an outdoor Collie
I get a pat on the head
I'm not used to cuddles or being taken to bed.

I'm a really nice Collie if given the time
To make the transition
To your world from mine.
© *Protecting Preloved Border Collies*

Experienced fosterers needed with outside space if you can help please contact us protectingprelovedbordercollies@yahoo.com

Editor's Note

Lee Montgomery-Hughes

Website: http://leemontgomery.weebly.com

Thank you for reading the second in the series of books promoting the work of Protecting Preloved Border Collies rescue.

It is far too often that the media portray only the darker side of animal neglect, the cruelty and abuse cases but all rescues cover so much more. The idea behind the book(s) was to try and show the crazy, fun and rewarding side to being part of a rescue network.

A BIG shout-out needs to go to the people directly involved as everything contained in this book comes from the people involved, and is written in their own words. I would like to thank them all for the contributions and photos as without their enthusiasm for this project it would never have happened.

Hopefully after reading this you will have been inspired to join the ever-growing team of fosterers, transporters, and fundraisers. If so please do not hesitate to contact PPBC ... they would love to hear from you.

However, it is also appreciated that not everyone is in a position to make that kind of commitment, but you can still help though simply promoting and raising awareness of the rescue.

Printed in Great
Britain
by Amazon